Experiencing the Trinity...

Is <u>One</u> a Lonely Number?

David G. Frantz

ISBN 979-8-89043-925-3 (paperback)
ISBN 979-8-89043-926-0 (digital)

Christian Faith Publishing
832 Park Avenue
Meadville, PA 16335
www.christianfaithpublishing.com

Printed in the United States of America

Figure 1. *The Trinity* by Andrei Rublev, fifteenth
century (Tretyakov Gallery, Moscow)

In memory of Norman Heaney, PhD (1914–1996),
and Charles Willson Rector, PhD (1926–2023)

Contents

Preface

In a world currently divided by violent discord, disharmony, and uncompromising factions, perhaps it is time to take a fresh look at the peace that God offers us—a time of quiet reflection on three major gifts, beginning with creation. Creation is first discussed in Genesis and continues through all time to bring evidence of God's love in the beauty of nature and the joy we receive from such bounty. Next is recognizing the blessings of redemption for all human shortcomings—for things done and left undone, for sins committed knowingly or unknowingly against our fellowman—resulting in the gift of unconditional forgiveness, which is lovingly and unceasingly granted. And the last is seeking sanctification through the assistance of a counselor or intercessor to strengthen, reinforce, and guide all persons in their daily lives to a more peaceful and righteous way of life. These gifts are available to all.

This then is the purpose of the book: to provide to all the faithful a tangible means to assist in obtaining peace, rest, and reassurance through a more personal relationship with the Trinity. By reducing the complexity and mystery associated with the Trinity, the author endeavors to provide

an easily understood approach to the subject, as substanti-
ated by scripture and further interpreted by historical and
contemporary commentary. Moreover, the customary path
of communication with the Trinity is briefly reviewed in
the "Conclusion" section as a reminder of how easily the
door is opened.

Introduction

For centuries, theologians, historians, and others have debated the legitimacy, substance, function, and placement of the Trinity in the practice of the Christian faith. This book attempts to set forth an easily understood explanation of what the Trinity may be, how it may function as an integral part of Christian worship, and the possible role it plays in the everyday consciousness of believing Christians. Because of its complexities, the discussions will not include an exhaustive review of its extremely long historical evolution or the many, many interpolations that have evolved over the centuries. The humble attempt here is to set forth a simple lay approach to the subject that will assist individuals, perhaps even provoke individuals, to deeper thought as they reflect on their weekly recitation of the Nicene Creed and/or the Apostles Creed during worship.

To enhance simplicity, consistency, and clarity, all scripture references in the discussion will be from *The Ryrie Study Bible (NIV)* by Charles Caldwell Ryrie. The author of this book has been engaged in a serious active study of scripture since 1991, and this version of the Bible has been utilized throughout.

One of the most popular visible depictions of the Trinity is the icon created in the fifteenth century by the Russian iconographer Andrei Rublev. The original is still displayed at the Tretyakov Gallery in Moscow. It is beyond the scope of this book to review the myriad interpretations of the icon; however, there is one important aspect relevant to the theme of this book. That is the social gesture depicted, wherein all three subjects are gently inclined toward one another while partaking from a common bowl or chalice. Of note also are Christ's two fingers apparently indicating "that he has put spirit and matter, divinity and humanity, together within himself—and for us!"[1] In addition, the Holy Spirit is indicating with his right hand that there may be an empty fourth space at the table. Is that for us?

The respected contemporary theologian Richard Rohr muses that if the icon is taken seriously, one can assert, "In the beginning was the Relationship," another important theme of this book. It is also interesting to note that this icon is mentioned by many theologians as the defining depiction of the Trinity—yet not including the "dove" that many acknowledge as the representation of the Holy Spirit. As for that matter, why is Christ in the middle, not God, with Christ seated at the right hand of God the Father? A color copy of the icon is presented immediately after the book's title page.

Proceeding now to the discussion of the book, it will cover the following: first, the *objections* to the Trinity, which have evolved over the centuries, in this case outlining several traditional misconceptions, inaccuracies, or questionable misinterpretations of the Trinity; second, the *origins* of the relationships inherent in the three elements of the Trinity; third, a brief but perhaps presumptuous comment on the individual "elements," their respective characterizations, and the dynamics of their interrelationships; fourth, the identifications of various *manifestations* of the three elements through time; fifth, and finally, the *conclusions*, including most importantly an answer to the question posed in the title.

The contents of the book represent almost thirty years of reflection and study on the subject. The compilation of notes and thoughts in the book reflects a true labor of love, with deep gratitude to the group of men who inspired the project and contributed mightily to the inspiration resulting in the author. The book is dedicated to the memory of Norman Heaney and Charles Rector. Norman Heaney was the founder and first leader of the group of men, and Charles Rector was one of the earliest members. Coincidentally, both men obtained PhDs from Johns Hopkins University, the former in economics and the latter in physics. Both men were profound scholars of scripture.

Objections

There are two fundamental assumptions that underpin or form the foundation for this book: First, God created mankind "in our own image, in our own likeness,"[2] and with the perfect exercise of free will. Second, all scripture in the Bible is "divinely inspired"[3] and is only imperfected by the original transcribers.

At the onset, a list of objections is presented. These objections will identify several prominent arguments against the Trinity doctrine. Initially, the book will discuss the basis of these respective denials.

1. The word *trinity* does not appear anywhere in the Scriptures, including both the Old and New Testaments; therefore, it is not a valid teaching in Scripture. The defense is that just because a specific doctrine or teaching in Scripture is not identified or given a precise appellation in Scripture does not in itself invalidate it.

2. Testimony of Hebrew Scriptures bears no clear teaching of the Trinity in the first thirty-nine books of the Bible that make up the true canon of the

Hebrew Scriptures. The defense here, of course, is that there are no revelations or indications in the Old Testament since the doctrine was openly identified in the New Testament with the Incarnation and Pentecost! However, there are inferences as indicated in the second chapter including Martin Luther's "prefigurings".

3. The testimony of the Greek Scriptures, apart from omitting a direct reference to the Trinity, contains no clear teaching of the doctrine in the canon of twenty-seven books comprising the New Testament. In this instance, nothing could be more false because the book of John contains detailed and repeated references as well as in the other Gospels, including Paul's writings.

4. Early Christians did not teach or consider the Trinity a doctrine. While not with great precision, there are many references in Paul's letters, as well as examples in the third and fourth centuries of philosophers and theologians pondering the subject and even writing about it. References to these teachers and writers will be indicated later in the book.

5. The doctrine of the Trinity is purely speculative and therefore superfluous! Many early writers and theologians have questioned the doctrine as a practical truth. Kant complains "From the doctrine of the Trinity, taken literally nothing whatsoever can be gained for practical purposes, even if one believed that one comprehended it—and less still if one is conscious that it surpasses all other

concepts."[4] This assertion is contrary to the literal interpretation of scripture and does not deserve further comment.

6. Among the recent theologians who are critical of the doctrine, Cyril C. Richardson asserts, "The doctrine of the Trinity is not a biblical doctrine....rather it is a creation of the fourth-century church."[5] He makes this assertion in the context that the perceptions of the original writers of Scripture were not precise, nor should modern theologians simply accept and report uncritically the thoughts they articulated. He goes on to assert that "we should not feel bound by their (original writers) particular symbolism if we find it at times detracts from or confuses the basic message it sought to convey."[6] This suggests the possibility of a canon within a canon—a criterion by which evolution and selection of biblical symbols are made, according to Millard J. Erickson in his study, *God in Three Persons.*[7] Here, one discovers the basic danger of revisionist thinkers and writers. That is to say, they start down a spiraling descent from what occurred or was actually written and witnessed about the facts as they originally occurred. Hence, the record is distorted by interpretations rather than by enlightened revelation!

7. Another contemporary theologian, Harnack, occupied himself with the overall general notion that "the revelation of God is limited to his Fatherhood" and that Christ, as the bearer of this revelation, fulfilled his only true purpose. Worse, "the Gospel

as Jesus proclaimed has to do with the Father only and not with the Son.[8] In Erickson's discussion of Harnack's thesis, he asserts that Harnack apparently believed Jesus had nothing to say about himself except to associate himself with all men in his relationship with the Father.[9] The suggestion is that any customary understanding of relationship within the Trinity is dissolved in favor of generalized father-son relationships of all persons to God and therefore completely discounting the doctrine of the Trinity. Such assertion obviously refutes the accounts of the original Scripture writers and represents a total refutation of their writings and very lives!

8. Finally, a whole body of subordinationism theology has emerged over the centuries, which, in its context, has included the gender issue in more recent times, principally in the latter twentieth century. A thorough discussion of this theology is far beyond the scope of this book. However, a brief survey of this doctrine is included at the end of chapter IV, "Dynamics." (Subordinationism is generally defined by the belief that the Son of God and the Holy Spirit are eternally set under the Father.)

Regardless of the progressing acceptance of neuter or feminist evolution relative to God's masculine image, the original writers of Scripture are quite clear and consistent in their pronouncement of this image. Apparently, since the Augustine interpretation, the patriarchal model has dominated and remains so at this point in Christian history. Three of the major religions today—Christianity, Judaism, and Islam—do not have a feminine deity of any kind. However, that said, Erickson, in his definitive book on the subject, asserts that the God of Christian revelation should not be thought of as either male or female. He is particularly critical of those who depict God the Father in patriarchal terms. He goes on to state, "God is not bound by gender or sex; he transcends both. It is quite possible that the Patriarchal depiction of God that we find in much Christian theology is an illicit development of the masculine motifs in isolation from other qualities and from the biblical contexts in which they were originally given."[10] Of course, this notion is firmly supported with Christ's discussions of the widow's successive marriages of the seven brothers in Luke 20:35–36.

The above-identified criticisms represent only a cursory review of several of the more prominent such declarations, not only in the early centuries but also in more contemporary times. Despite the record, the early constructs, including the Council of Nicaea (325 CE), the Council of Constantinople (381 CE), and the early theologians, namely Tertullian (who actually coined the term *trinity*) and Origen, the Trinity Doctrine, have prevailed! Perhaps it was by divine intervention?

Origins

The following discussion will include a review of the scriptural origins of the Trinity.

As previously indicated, the true genesis of the Trinity presumably presents itself in the New Testament with the Incarnation and Pentecost. However, for centuries, scholars and theologians have preoccupied themselves with searching for clues or early indications foretelling the Trinity in the Old Testament.

Again, it is beyond the scope of this book to review all those precursor efforts. Suffice it to say, the God of Israel did reveal himself in the Old Testament as Father, Messiah, and Holy Spirit. One early incident is worth noting in Genesis 18. It involves the encounter between Abraham and the three men at Mamre. In the encounter, "Abraham looked up and saw three men standing nearby." In verse 3, he greeted them, "If I have found favor in your eyes, my Lord," interestingly in the first person singular! However, in verse 5, the three answered him: "'Very well,' they answered, 'do as you say.'"

During the subsequent conversation, *they* is used in the manuscript until verse 10, when the singular "Lord" is used to indicate the other person in the conversation. In subsequent chapters in Genesis, such personages are identified as "angel or angels of the Lord." Suffice it to say, given the strong proclivity of the Hebrews to be monotheistic in their belief and worship, there is no evidence literally in Scripture to indicate in the Old Testament that there exists more than one Deity. Note from the Shema of Deuteronomy 6:4–5, "Hear O Israel: The Lord our God, the Lord is one. Love the Lord your God with all your heart and with all your soul and with all your strength."[11]

However, before turning to the New Testament references, it is worth noting Martin Luther's interpretation of the "prefigurings" of the Trinity in the general context of his exegesis of the Old Testament. According to Mickey Mattox in his excellent book on the subject, Luther turned his attention to a text very few today, or even in his own day, would have chosen as a basis for a defense of the Trinitarian context in Scripture.[12] In 2 Samuel 23:1–3, David's last words, there exists a clear identification of God, the Holy Spirit, and perhaps of Christ, sufficient that Luther used this passage in his urging that the Catholic doctrines of the Trinity needed reemphasis as well as renewed recognition. Specifically, Mattox points out that a literal reading of the text indicated to Luther that the Holy Spirit here introduces, in the words *God* and *rock*, both the Father and the Son. Luther's consideration of this reference was in the context of

the advance in Hebrew studies that he wanted to retain, in spite of the difficulties these studies admittedly caused, considering that in a grammatical analysis that showed the diversity of divine names used here and elsewhere in the Hebrew text should not be understood as instances of a superfluity of words, but as precious textural intimations-clear to the Christian-of the Triune God.[13]

In addition, throughout his analysis of the Old Testament, Luther indicated a general principle that wherever two of the divine persons are mentioned, "you may boldly assume that the three persons of the Godhead are there indicated."[14]

Besides 2 Samuel 23, Luther relied on Psalm 2 (particularly Psalm 110), Genesis 1:26, Genesis 4:1, 2 Samuel 7, and Daniel 7, as well as Isaiah, in his "prefigurings" to justify the Trinity and the two natures in Christ (God and Holy Spirit) in the Old Testament. His attention to and deep convictions about the Trinity "prefigurings" were prompted by his defense of Catholic teachings on the subject, particularly during the period following the publication of the 1541 revision of the Luther Bible in preparation for the 1545 edition, the last published during his lifetime. Perhaps the most succinct summary of Luther's Trinitarian theology is contained in his lecture to his students on Genesis 1:26 in 1535:

Therefore here (i.e., in Gen 1:26) the Trinity is clearly signified, that in the one divine essence there are three persons, Father, Son, and Holy Spirit; thus not even with regard to activity (of creation) is God separated, for all three persons here agree together and say "let us make." The Father does not make any other man than the Son, nor the Son than the Holy Spirit, but the Father, Son, and Holy Spirit, one in the same.

God, is the author and creator of the same work. Thus, neither in this way can God be separated as a thing present to the mind (objective). For God the Father is not known, except in the Son and through the Holy Spirit. Therefore, just as with regard to activity (i.e., Creation) so also is a thing present to the mind of God is one, who nevertheless within himself substantively or essentially is Father, Son, Holy Spirit, three distinct persons in one divinity.[15]

As Mattox points out in this context, for Luther, God the Creator is a Trinity of divine persons whose works are indivisible. He, Mattox, further asserts, "The revelation of God the Father in the Son through the Holy Spirit is therefore a revelation of God as God is."

Luther also provides an instructive segue to the New Testament manifestations of the Trinity in his *Large Catechism* (*LC*) written in 1529. The document, some five pages long, served as a guide for the new Protestant "evangelical" churches being established in Saxony (1525). It included Luther's summation of the Ten Commandments, the Apostles' Creed, and brief interpretations of each article.

His subjective experience of the Triune God and his understanding of the concept are nowhere made clearer than in the LC, particularly in his exposition of the Apostles' Creed. Mattox asserts that the creed "is a word of grace that tells who God is and what God has done for us."[16]

In the first article of the *LC*, Luther emphasizes God as Creator. Therefore, it follows that to know God is to know self as a creature, one who is defined and whose limits have been determined by God. Luther asserts, "Thus we learn from this article that none of us has life—or anything else that has been mentioned here or can be mentioned—from ourselves, nor can we by ourselves preserve any of them, however small and unimportant."[17] Here, Luther's assertion seems to negate all idolatry, including all that is based on human works!

For example, does Ayn Rand's elaboration of the existentialism philosophy as contained in her books *Atlas Shrugged* and *The Fountainhead* come to mind? This fatherly function provides the human experience the path to appreciate God's provision for every aspect of human life as well as the requirement for thankfulness for his boundless blessings and "goodness." From Luther's perspective, acknowledging God as hereby revealed as well as confessed in the Creed, accepts him as the creator of all through his supreme benevolence.

In the second article, Luther addresses the "true" Son of God. As many theologians over the centuries have indicated, the remarkable aspect of this article is its brevity. Luther simply asserts that the Son has through his victory over sin, death, and evil graciously become "our Lord through his work as Redeemer." As Mattox points out, the emphasis from Luther is here subjective, in the sense that Luther portrays the Son, establishing himself as the redeemer by means of his saving work. Mattox further points out that other earlier theologians have asserted that apart from the brevity of this article, the work and person of the redeemer is only the starting point of Luther's Trinitarian theology. In essence, the knowledge of God for Luther is grounded first, last and always in the humanity of Christ. In summary, it is through the Son in his incarnate humanity that the way is opened to knowing God and the Holy Spirit. Hence, his very living among us is equally relevant to his ultimate sacrifice for us.

The bulk of Luther's exposition of the Apostles' Creed is directed to the third article, "Sanctification." From Luther's perspective, the ministry of the Holy Spirit is the starting point of Christian faith and life, since the Spirit brings the Christian to Christ and, through Christ, reveals the love of the Father. For Luther then, *sanctification* means simply being incorporated into Christ through our righteousness. He further thought that incorporation itself was impossible without the ministry of the Spirit in the church. This author would submit, however, that the church is not essential, that the Spirit continually indwells and acts within every one of us according to Christ's good purposes for our salvation. Again, from Luther's perspective of the Christian experience, the knowledge of God proceeds in the Spirit, through the Son, and ultimately to the Father. Luther further believed that as a manifestation of the living faith, one obtains "in the Apostles' Creed the entire essence, will, and work of God."[18]

Turning now to the New Testament, Millard Erickson, in his book *God in Three Persons*, presents an interesting assertion in the context of "doctrinal formulations." He specifies that there was no official creed in the earliest days of the church; however, some have claimed that the Apostles' Creed is actually attributed to Jesus's original intimate circle of twelve! Tyrannius Rufinus's writing, circa 404 CE, asserted that as the apostles were about to go their separate ways in their ministry following Pentecost, they decided they should agree on the basic content of the message. To minimize the divergence among them, they met at one spot, and under the filling of the Holy Spirit, each contributed a part they felt should be included. They then agreed on this content as the standard to be used in their teaching.[19]

Apparently, this general understanding continued into the Middle Ages. In the fifteenth century, however, disputes over this assertion broke out at the Council of Florence (1438–45) between the Latin church, which accepted the apostolic authority of the creed, and the Greek church, which did not. In the nineteenth century, the skepticism continued whether there was any creed at all or whether any organized body of doctrine could have existed in the New Testament period, since again, there was no direct reference in the text. Therefore, many critics have held, particularly in the early twentieth century, that there were no complete creeds in the early phase of the church and that they did not become a reality until such formulated creeds were developed in the middle of the second century.[20]

With respect to the Gospels, beginning with Matthew, specific references to the Trinity are literally indicated.

Perhaps the first clear expression of the concept of the Trinity is Matthew 3:16–17:

> As soon as Jesus was baptized...at that moment heaven was opened and he saw the Spirit of God descending like a dove and lighting on him. And a voice from heaven said' This is my son whom I love; with him I am well pleased.[21]

The second indication in Matthew is found in the Great Commission: Matthew 28:18–20, "All authority in heaven and on earth has been given to me. Therefore go... baptizing them in the name of the Father and of the Son and of the Holy Spirit."[22]

In Mark, the Trinity is reflected in the baptism, which occurs in Mark 1:9–11.

In Luke 1:35, the Holy Spirit is revealed in the preface to the Magnificat: "The Holy Spirit will come upon you, and the power of the Most High will overshadow you. So, the holy one to be born will be called the Son of God."

As the NIV indicates in a footnote to this verse,

> The Incarnation was accomplished by this creative act of the Holy Spirit in the body of Mary. The virgin birth was a special miracle performed by the third Person of the Trinity, the eternal Son of God, took to Himself a genuine though sinless human nature and was born as a

man without surrendering in any aspect
His deity.

Finally in Luke:24:49, the Trinity is revealed as Christ promises the Day of Pentecost: "I am going to send you what my Father has promised, but stay in the city until you have been clothed with power from on high."

In the most theological of the four Gospels, John is found to be the most complete revelation and discussion of the Trinity. As the NIV presents in its preface to the Gospel, it deals with the nature and person of Christ as well as the meaning of faith in him. In addition, it indicates his deity as asserted in the series of "I am" claims. In other "I am" statements, Christ made implicit and explicit the claim to be the I am Yahweh of the Old Testament (John 4:24, 26; 8:24, 28, 58; 13:19). These are the strongest claims to Deity that Jesus could have made. Also, John emphasizes the physical actuality of Jesus—that is, hunger, thirst, weariness, pain, and death—as a defense against the Gnostic denial of Jesus's true human nature.

From the very beginning of the Gospel of John, a very important fact is revealed. Known as "the preexistent Christ," the NIV footnote to the first verse of John indicates that in the Logo concept, *Word* is applied to Jesus, "who is all that God is and the expression of Him" (John 1:1, 14). In this verse, the Word (Christ) is said to be with God (i.e., in communion with and yet distinct from God and to be God (i.e., identical, in essence with God).[23] The footnote also indicates in John 1:3 that Christ was active in the work of creation. See also John 1:18: "No one has ever seen God but God the One and Only who is at the Father's side, has made him known." This revelation is soundly reiterated in John 8:58: "Before Abraham was born, I am!"

Then as one moves to the baptismal verses, John reveals the Holy Spirit in John 1:32–34. Erickson, in his book, further elaborates on this occurrence:

> Of all the Gospel accounts only John's has John the Baptist testifying to having seen the descent of the dove. Presumably, the Baptist's reference to "the one who sent me to baptize with water" refers to God the Father, much like the testimony of the Old Testament prophets. If this is the case, then we have a collection of these three. Indeed, even so the "Son of God" brings the three together in one context.[24]

Moving on to John 3:13, Jesus reveals again his origin: "No one has ever gone into heaven except the one who comes from heaven—the Son of Man." Then again in John 3:16, Jesus claims who sent him: "For God so loved the world that he gave his one and only Son, that whoever believes in him shall not perish but have eternal life." In John 5:17–47, Jesus asserts his authority, which he bases on His special relation with the Father! Furthermore, in John 6:46, Jesus reiterates his origin: "No one has seen the Father, except the one who is from God, only he has seen the Father." And again, Jesus asserts his origin in John 7:29: "You do not know him, but I know him because I am from him and he sent Me."

An important indication of the differentiation of separateness of the Father and the Son is contained in John 10:30, where Jesus asserts, "I and the Father are one." The footnote to the verse in the NIV clarifies a potential misconception that "the Father and Son are in perfect unity in their nature and actions but the neuter form of 'one' rules out the meaning that they are one person." Of course, John 17, "the Great Prayer" or the "Intercession of the Son of God," so gloriously elaborates on this distinction as well as their unity. Moreover, in John 17:24, Jesus emphasizes again his existence before creation: "Father, I want those you have given me to see my glory, the glory you have given me because you loved me before the creation of the world." And yet again, in John 20:17, Jesus reiterates his separateness from the Father by telling Mary Magdalene, "Go instead to my brothers and tell them, 'I am returning to my Father and your Father to my God and your God.'" In addition, this declaration should quiet the many assertions over the centuries that Christianity is not monotheistic but conceivably tritheistic. Finally, in John 20:22, Jesus reveals the Holy Spirit to the Apostles: "And he breathed on them and said, 'Receive the Holy Spirit.'" The NIV footnote indicates, "This was a filling of the Spirit for power until regularized relationship of the Spirit began at Pentecost."

There are numerous other references throughout Scripture to the three persons of the Trinity, but none are as complete or thorough as in John. One exception might be in the Pauline letters, where there are a number of passages where he mentions the three names together, as Erickson indicated in his book.[25]

Notably, in these references, in the benediction in 2 Corinthians 13:14, "May the grace of the Lord Jesus Christ, and the love of God, and the fellowship of the Holy Spirit be with you all." As Erickson indicates, "This is a close association of the three persons in a combined or at least coordinated working (the conferring of blessings) that suggests equal status. It is presented as if they all have the right to do this."[26]

In addition, within Romans, Paul's most theological or doctrinal book, there are a number of references to the three persons in the Trinity, including their separate, distinct roles yet their interdependence. Noted also is the fact that the Holy Spirit receives a more complete treatment by Paul in Romans 8 than anywhere else in Scripture, with the exception of the lengthy discussion by Jesus in John 14–16. Here, it is clear that Paul regards the Holy Spirit as a person, with his role as an intercessor; in this context, note Romans 8:9–11.

Concluding this chapter, several revelations are presented in a literal review of the Scriptures:

1. In a number of instances, there is more than ample evidence presented that Christ existed with God (his Father) before creation.

2. Without becoming preoccupied with the nuances and disparate translations from different languages (i.e., Hebrew, Aramaic, Latin, Greek, and English), there exist three distinct "persons" within the Godhead. Moreover, the three persons exist in a nonhierarchal arrangement, perhaps codependent and constantly interacting with one another in eternity.

3. Christ was revealed to the world through the Incarnation, and he, in turn, revealed the Holy Spirit to mankind at Pentecost and on Easter evening when Jesus breathed on the Apostles and said, "Receive the Holy Spirit" (John 20:22). However, the Holy Spirit may have existed before creation as well (Genesis 1:2) and was directly involved in the Incarnation (Luke 1:35).

4. In the Judeo-Christian ethos, believers are monotheistic (even Christologists), and based on the above presentation, including Christ's own testimony, there is emphatic evidence to refute any notion of tritheism.

Dynamics

Turning now to a comment on the interactive forces of the three persons: Volumes have been written on the subject over the centuries, so this discussion will only serve to elaborate in a cursory fashion on how these forces relate to the intent of this book.

God

God is the omnipotent creator of the world and the Father of his Son, Jesus Christ. Sufficient for this book, he is acknowledged and worshiped from the time of Moses's great declaration, the Shema.

Jesus Christ

The eternal Son of God, who existed before creation, was revealed to mankind at the Incarnation. His life and ministry were equally important to his ultimate sacrifice for all the sins of the world. Beginning in the very first verse of Hebrews 1:1–3:

> In the past, God spoke to our forefathers through the prophets at many times and in various ways, but in these last days he has spoken to us by his Son, whom he appointed heir of all things, and through whom he made the universe. The Son is the radiance of God's glory and the exact representation of his beginning, sustaining all things by his powerful word. After he had provided purification for sins, he sat down at the right hand of the Majesty in heaven.

Subsequently, in Hebrews 9:15, the author of the letter to the Hebrews declares,

> For this reason, Christ is the mediator of a new covenant that those who are called may receive the promised eternal inheritance—now that he has died as a ransom to set them free from the sins committed under the first covenant.

A footnote in the NIV for Philippians 2:7 from Paul's writings reveals additional key information about Christ's personage:

> The Kenosis (emptying) of Christ during the Incarnation does not mean that

He surrendered any attributes of deity, but that He took on the limitations of humanity. This involved a veiling of His preincarnate glory (John 7:5) and the voluntary waiving of some of His divine prerogatives during the time He was on earth (Matt. 24:36).

Furthermore, the author of Hebrews declared in Hebrews 8:13, "By calling this covenant 'new' he (God) has made the first one (the Laws) obsolete; and what is obsolete, and aging will soon disappear." One could deduce from this declaration that having created mankind with a "perfect exercise of free will," it was difficult to follow the letter of the law, day by day, just as in today's world it seems impossible for all to obey speed signs.

Therefore, God's first covenant could be deemed his "failed experiment," and from the Episcopal *Book of Common Prayer*,

> Again and again you called us to return, through prophets and sages you revealed your righteous Law. And in the fullness of time, you sent your only Son, born of a woman, to fulfill your Law, to open for us the way of freedom and peace.[27]

The Holy Spirit

As previously indicated, Jesus reveals the Holy Spirit at Pentecost and on the evening of the first day of Easter. However, in John 1:32–34, John the Baptist also testifies,

> I saw the Spirit come down from heaven as a dove and remain on him. I would not have known him, except that the one who sent me to baptize with water told me "The man on whom you see the Spirit come down and remain is he who will baptize with the Holy Spirit" I have and I testify that this is the Son of God.

As previously indicated, the most complete treatment of the Holy Spirit occurs in John and the Romans. In John 4:26, the origin and function of the Holy Spirit are indicated: "But the Counselor, the Holy Spirit, whom the Father will send in my name will teach you all things and will remind you of everything I have said to you." As Erickson points out,

> Here something of the inner relationships within the Trinity is revealed. The father does the sending of the Holy Spirit but does so in the name of the Son. The Spirit will remind Jesus' followers of the words of Jesus.[28]

Erickson goes on to emphasize that Jesus identifies the Counselor as the Holy Spirit; therefore, unless the Counselor is mentioned elsewhere in Scripture, it is clear to whom he is referring. In John 16:7, he says, "It is for your good that I am going away. Unless I go away the Counselor will not come to you; but if I go, I will send him to you." Note here that not only will the Father send the Spirit, but Jesus also will. The same message is indicated previously in John 14:15–16: "If you love me, you will obey what I command. And I will ask the Father, and he will give you another Counselor, to be with you forever—the Spirit of Truth."

In Romans 8:6, Paul elaborates on the functions of the Spirit: "The mind of sinful man is death, but the mind controlled by the Spirit is life and peace." In Romans 8:11, "And if the Spirit of him, who raised Jesus from the dead is living in you, he who raised Christ from the dead will also give life to your mortal bodies through his Spirit who lives in you." Finally, in Romans 8:26, "In the same way, the Spirit helps us in our weakness. We do not know what we ought to pray for, but the Spirit himself intercedes for us with groans that words cannot express." The footnote from the NIV further elaborates, "The Holy Spirit helps our weakness (our inability to pray intelligently about situations)…Such intercession is in accord with God's will." Erickson concludes his treatment of the subject by asserting:

> We need to note that the Holy Spirit is a person, with all the qualities of a person. He exercises a personal ministry in the lives of persons. He does the connect-

ing and convincing of unbelievers-of sin, of righteousness, and of judgement (John 16:8–11). He regenerates or gives new life (John 3:5–8). He guides into truth (John 16:13). He inspired the Scripture writers to produce the books of the Bible as we have them. He sanctifies believers (Rom. 8:1–77). He empowers for service (Acts 1:8). We are not told that in any of these works he does what he does through the Father or the Son. These are direct ministries involving a direct relationship.[29]

Concluding this chapter, there has apparently been an assertion over the centuries among theologians that there exists a distinction among the three members of the Trinity. For instance, in Mark 10:18, Jesus refers to himself as a teacher and declares, "No one is good—but God alone." Without delving into the vagaries of definitions surrounding "personhood" or person, Scripture reveals throughout that members are "one heart and one mind," and *verbatim* in Acts 4:32.

In one of the most beautiful chapters of the Bible, John 17, Jesus asserts that consciously, the three are one—that the three perfectly share goals, intentions, objectives, and values. Apparently, the three are eternally and permanently one with the other. As Erickson asserts, "The linkage and interdependence within the Trinity are such that there could not be a living God, nor could there be a Father, Son, or Spirit without each of the others."[30] This spiritual and social dynamic will be developed in the succeeding chapter, relying specifically on contemporary theologians, which perhaps can assist in bringing relevance to more current societal implications.

Before leaving the discussion of dynamics, it is useful to address the question of the Trinity and "subordinationism." *Subordinationism* is defined as the belief that the Son of God and the Holy Spirit are eternally set under the Father (God). As early as the fourth century, the debate on this subject raged principally between the early theologians Arius and Athanasius. Arius, a third-century theologian from Alexandria, espoused the notion that the Son of God was not truly God in human flesh. He held in the Greek understanding of God that God is a pure spirit who can have no direct contact with the material world.

As Kevin Giles points out in his thorough discussion of the subject, for Arius, "the Son of God must be a secondary God, different in being or substance from the Father."[31] As Giles further points out, Arius further argued that because the Son is subordinated eternally in his being/essence, he was also subordinated in his works or role to the Father.

At the Council of Nicaea in 325 CE, as we now know, the assembled bishops rejected Arius's teaching, insisting the Son was "one being or substance (Greek "homoiousious") with the Father. The one theologian who initially led the refutation of Arius's theory was Athanasius. For Athanasius, the difference of the members of the Trinity does not imply subordination. Giles emphasizes this point by citing Scripture that tells about the Father and the Son being "one" and about their each abiding in the other (John 10:30, 38; 14:10–11; 17:21).[32]

It is also important as Giles emphasizes that the unity of being and action among the Father, Son, and Holy Spirit cannot be separated. Unlike humans, Giles further asserts, "Who the triune God is (his being) and what the triune does (his acts) are one." Joining Athanasius in his refutation of the subordinationism theology, besides the Cappadocian fathers (during his lifetime),[33] were subsequently Augustine, Calvin, the creeds and confessions, and most contemporary theologians.

The Cappadocian Fathers were all born in Asia Minor, and two of whom were brothers. They consisted of Basil of Caesarea, known as "the Great"; his brother Gregory of Nyssa; and their mutual friend, Gregory of Nazianzus, a poet and orator. They all lived in the latter fourth century and were particularly noted for their contributions to early Trinity theology. The discussions taken at the Council of Constantinople in 381 CE were, in large measure, the results of the work of the Cappadocian Fathers. It was this council that reaffirmed the doctrine of Nicaea regarding the divinity of the Son as well as the Holy Spirit. Hence, it was this council that definitively proclaimed the doctrine of the Trinity.

Essentially, the primary contribution of the Cappadocian Fathers was in clarifying the difference between *ousis* ("essence") and *hypostasis*, which literally means "substance," but which the fathers defined as the translation of Latin *persons*. Hence, the Latin West and the Greek East came to agree on a common formula: one essence in three persons, or "hypostases."[34]

In further developing Athanasius's thinking, they underlined the distinction of the divine three in differing relationships based upon their eternal origins: the Father "unbegotten," the Son "begotten," and the Spirit "proceeding." The Cappadocian Fathers spoke of the Father as the "sole" source or sole origin of the Son and Spirit. However, the Son and the Spirit shared equally in one being with the Father, the "homoiousious" of the Father. The take-away from this discussion is that, beginning primarily with Athanasius, all members of the Trinity are eternally one in "being" and "doing." Asserting here that the Son, present at creation with the Father, willingly and gladly subordinated himself temporarily for us, only in the incarnation did the Son assume an inferior or subordinate status for our salvation!

Manifestations

As Giles indicated in his study, the doctrine of the Trinity has been the foremost concern of theologians in two periods of the church's history: the fourth century and the latter part of the twentieth century, leading into the twenty-first century. Turning now to more contemporary considerations, one of the most significant conclusions of Millard Erickson is his emphasis on the communion relationship of the Trinity members:

> The Trinity is a communion of three persons, three centers of consciousness, who exist and always have existed in union with one another. Each is dependent for his life on each of the others. They share their lives, having such a close relationship that each is conscious of what the other is conscious of. They have never had any prior independent existence and will not and cannot have any such now or in the future....They are bound to one another in love, agape love, which therefore unites

them in the closest and most intimate of relationships.[35]

Two other noted contemporary theologians have developed this same theme: Jürgen Moltmann in his work, *The Trinity and the Kingdom*, and most recently Richard Rohr in his work, *The Divine Dance*.

Moltmann summarizes his conclusion in the notion of a "social doctrine of the Trinity," wherein God is a community of Father, Son, and Spirit whose unity is constituted by "mutual indwelling" and "reciprocal interpenetration." He ultimately reaches the conclusion of this divine sociality: "not in the autocracy of a single ruler, but in the democratic community of free people, not in the lordship of the man over the woman, but in their equal mutuality, not in an ecclesiastical hierarchy but in a fellowship church."[36]

While some of Moltmann's assertions appear to be contrary to some of Paul's teachings, his emphasis on freedom and the "perfect exercise of free will" is consistent with one of the basic assumptions of this book, particularly that it emphasizes the notion that mankind was created in God's image. In the context of the Trinity, he elaborates

> that the Kingdom of the Father is determined by the creation of the world and its presentation through God's patience. This constitutes the freedom of created things… The Kingdom of the Son is determined by the liberation of men and women through suffering love. This restores the freedom of created beings and redeems them from

self-destruction. The Kingdom of the Spirit finally, is determined by the powers and energies of the new creation.[37]

All of this directly reflects the purposes and manifestations of the New Covenant with God and its ultimate actualization in modern life.

One of the most recent books on the socialization of the Trinity is Rohr's book. He elaborates throughout the book on the richness of human life that flows constantly from the Trinity (all three personages)! In this marvelous work, he brings to the human experience the dynamic manifestations of each member of the Trinity and then their collective manifestation in the "divine dance." He summarizes his declaration in a prayer:

> God for us, we call you Father. God alongside us, we call you Jesus. God within us, we call you Holy Spirit. You are the eternal mystery that enables, enfolds, and enlivens all things, even us, even me. Every name falls short of your goodness and greatness. We can only see who you are in what is. We ask for such perfect seeing—As it was in the beginning, is now and ever shall be. Amen.[38]

Rohr asserts that Jesus is "God alongside us," accompanying God who walks with us "through the mystery of death and resurrection of letting go and receiving." In essence, this is the living manifestation—the Christ, the best direct and concise summary of all Jesus's teachings and experience. He further asserts that "life has no real opposite; death is merely a transition which takes trust every time we walk through it."[39] Finally, Rohr asserts the Holy Spirit as the dynamism within and between the Father and the Son. He contends that the "indwelling Spirit is the constant and continuing ability of humanity to keep going, to keep recovering from its wounds, to keep hoping, to keep recovering." Rohr concludes this notion of the Trinity by stating, "Thus if God the Father is the Un-manifest, then the Christ is the original movement in Manifestation. The more open you are to the Holy Spirit's prompting and invitations, the wider your seeing becomes."[40] Rohr quotes another noted contemporary theologian, Frank Viola, to reiterate his fundamental description of the Trinity and its manifestation:

> Within the triune God we discover mutual love, mutual fellowship, mutual dependence, mutual honor, mutual submission, mutual dwelling and authentic community. In the Godhead, there exists an eternal, complimentary and reciprocal interchange of divine life, divine love, and divine fellowship...The church is an organic extension of the triune God.[41]

Finally, Rohr concludes his thesis in his own words:

> You are the desiring of God, God desires all things in and through you. And if you're feeling any desire for God grow-

ing as you read these pages, this is the Son's desire for fellowship with the Father acting itself out in and through you. This is the Holy Spirit who is the personification of the eternal and abundant energy, life, and love between the other two. Listen to this desiring and wait for its deeper-deepest level. It will get you there as the Holy Spirit always does.[42]

Rohr asserts in his closing thoughts that once he was able to move from pyramid thinking to circular thinking because of the Trinity, his mind let go of its own defenses and stopped refusing the universal dance—hence the title of his book!

So the final chapter of this book's research and contemplation is concluded. It is fitting that it focused on the writings—thought patterns of contemporary theologians. It does not include the results of historical development or continuous debates on the subject, which have evolved over the centuries and continue today. Its contents reflect sentiments or positions, after a great deal of research on the subject, that perhaps most closely reflect the ultimate conclusions of the book's author. Moreover, the thoughts may reflect a more easily understood or applicable reference for consideration in today's society of confusion, apathy, or even more seriously, refutation of the Trinity.

Conclusions

The answer to the question is most assuredly yes! God never intended for each individual he creates to be alone—for that matter, no creature at all. Having created humankind in his likeness, he was never alone, even before creation. The Scripture more than sufficiently indicates that his Son was with him and presumably the Holy Spirit as well before creation (Genesis 1:2), and quite possibly many other angels as well. The human experience from time immemorial has been one of social communion, dynamic interaction, and mutual sharing, including mere survival, especially during the earliest times. Only under the most unusual circumstances is an individual born with a proclivity or predilection to be alone and spend the duration of life on earth in isolation, removed from social interaction.

Therefore, it is certainly not surprising that God reveals to mankind his true nature and his "mastermind alliance" that has accompanied him throughout eternity. In the beginning, he established his "righteous law" through Moses and the prophets to govern behavior for his human creation. Because he created humans with the "perfect exercise of free will," he discovered that his human creation simply cannot consistently follow rules and laws, even today! Hence, "and in the fullness of time, he sent his only Son, born of a woman, to fulfill the Law, 'to open for us the way of freedom and peace.'"

The Episcopal *Book of Common Prayer* goes on to declare, "In him you have delivered us from evil, and made us worthy to stand before you. In him, you have brought us out of error into truth, out of sin into righteousness, out of death into life." All of this is accomplished in the New Covenant, with its sole foundation of love. Throughout the transmission of the New Covenant, God continued to reveal himself through the life and teachings of his Son and the continuing of those teachings by the energy of the Holy Spirit. Consequently, the Trinity exists! It is not debatable and seems unbelievable that the debate has endured, even to this day, apparently persisting among some large Christian denominations.

What is debatable, of course, is how the Trinity manifests itself, how the participants interact, and how they complement one another in their respective influences upon humankind. The whole subject of "subordinationism" continues to this day, even with apparent resolution in scripture. For the purposes of this book, the author finds it difficult to accept the hierarchical notion even though the three may affect their respective influences separately as indicated in the scriptural prescription (creation by the Father, redemption by the Son, and sanctification by the Spirit). The evidence appears to be overwhelming in scripture, namely, that in fact, "they are three in one," existing in three separate personages throughout eternity.

Finally, this all leads to a very brief comment on prayer. According to the Scripture, the Son instructs humankind not only to pray to God but also how to pray to him (i.e., the Lord's Prayer). Presumably and consequently, prayer should be directed to God rather than to other members of the Trinity, who must forward it to the Father. As a parenthetical, this whole discussion probably reverts all the way back to the differences between the moderate and more radical wings of the Reformation. The point being here, the less radical reformers, such as the Lutherans, "felt justified in retaining anything not explicitly prohibited in Scripture." That said, there is no command by Christ or anyone else in Scripture for people to pray to him. Normally, people do not think of prayer in the context of being made to someone who is physically present. However, with respect to the risen Lord, there is an entirely different circumstance.

When Stephen was being stoned to death, he prayed to the Lord, "Lord Jesus, receive my spirit" (Acts 7:8), and "Lord, do not hold this sin against them" (Acts 7:60). Moreover, Saul and Ananias both had conversations with Jesus. Throughout Paul's subsequent writings, he indicates he had many conversations or prayers with the Lord Jesus! Another beautiful passage of Scripture, Matthew 11:28–30, indicates that an invitation is extended for a relationship and interchange with Jesus.

Today, the Trinity is acknowledged and worshiped in the recitation of the creeds in houses of worship throughout the world. Communication with the Trinity is always available at all times and in all places through thoughtful, deliberate prayer. It may be as simple as directly repeating the Lord's Prayer, or it may be more involved with the special needs or concerns of the individual. Most importantly, God and Christ are always ready to hear the appeals of their creation, including the requisite gratefulness for all blessings endlessly received. The Counselor is ever present and ready to assist in the transmission of prayer!

Acknowledgments

I am deeply grateful to my family for their support and encouragement throughout the project. Special thanks to my wife for countless reviews, suggestions, and transcriptions over the months, leading to the ultimate decision to seek publication. Credit also is due to our younger son, who graciously took time from his studies at the US Naval War College to undertake the initial formatting. Finally, again a most heartfelt thanks to the group of men who inspired me over a number of years to undertake such a spiritual journey.

Notes

1   Richard Rohr, *The Divine Dance* (New Kensington, PA, 2016), p. 30.
2   *The Ryrie Study Bible: NIV* (Chicago, 1986); Gen. 1:26.
3   Ibid; 2 Tim. 3:16.
4   *Kant Im Streit Der Fakultaten*, PHB 252, p. 34.
5   Cyril C. Richardson, *The Doctrine of the Trinity* (Nashville, 1958), p. 17.
6   Ibid, p. 17.
7   Millard J. Erickson, *God in Three Persons* (Grand Rapids, 1995), p. 100.
8   Adolf Harnack, *What Is Christianity?* (New York, 1957), p. 144.
9   Erickson, p. 121
10 Ibid, p. 281.
11 Bible NIV, Deut. 6, Jesus Christ called this the "first and great commandment, and added to it the phrase "with all your mind" Mk. 12:30.
12 Mickey L. Mattox, "From Faith to the Text and Back Again: Martin Luther on the Trinity in the Old Testament" (Marquette University, 2006), p. 294.
13 Ibid, p. 299.
14 Ibid, p.300.
15 Ibid, p.286.
16 Ibid, p. 290.
17 Ibid, p. 290.
18 Ibid, p. 293.

[19] Erickson, p. 176.
[20] Erickson, p. 187.
[21] Bible NIV, Mat. 3:16–17.
[22] Ibid, Mat. 28:18–20.
[23] Bible NIV, Jn 1:1.
[24] Erickson, p. 205.
[25] Ibid, pp. 185–188.
[26] Ibid, p. 185.
[27] The Episcopal Church, *The Book of Common Prayer 1976* (Kingsport, TN, 1977), p. 370.
[28] Erickson, p. 206.
[29] Ibid, p. 327.
[30] Ibid, p. 233.
[31] Kevin Giles, *The Trinity and Subordinationism* (Downers Grove, IL, 2002), p. 13.
[32] Ibid, p. 13.
[33] Ibid, p. 14.
[34] Justo L. Gonzalez, *The Story of Christianity*, Vol I. (New York, NY, 2010), p. 217.
[35] Erickson, p.331.
[36] Juergen Moltmann, *The Trinity and the Kingdom* (Minneapolis, 1993), p. Vii.
[37] Ibid, p. 212.
[38] Rohr, p. 144.
[39] Ibid, p.169.
[40] Ibid, p.145.
[41] Frank Viola, *Reimaging Church: Pursuing the Dream of Organic Christianity* (Colorado Springs, 2008), p. 35.
[42] Rohr, p. 179.

Bibliography

Bourgeault, Cynthia. *The Holy Trinity and the Law of Three.* Boulder, CO: Shambhala Publications, Inc., 2013.

Erickson, Millard J. *God in Three Persons.* Grand Rapids, MI: Baker Books, 1995.

Giles, Kevin. *The Trinity and Subordinationism.* Downers Grove, IL: InterVarsity Press, 2002.

Gonzalez, Justo L. *The Story of Christianity.* Vol. I, II. New York, NY: Harper Brothers, 2010.

Harnack, Adolf von. *What Is Christianity?* New York, NY: Harper Brothers, 1957.

Kant, Immanuel. *Der Streit der Fakultaten.* Hamburg, Germany: Falix Meiner, 1975.

LaCugna, Catherine Mowry. *God for Us.* San Francisco, CA: Harper Collins, 1991.

Mattox, Mickey. "From Faith to the Text and Back Again: Martin Luther on the Trinity and the Old Testament." *Pro Ecclesia.* Vol. 15, No. 3: pp. 281–303. Marquette Un., Milwaukee, WI, 2006.

Moltmann, Jurgen. *The Trinity and the Kingdom.* Minneapolis, MN: First Fortress Press, 1993.

Richardson, Cyril C. *The Doctrine of the Trinity*. Nashville, TN: Abingdon, 1958.

Rohr, Richard. *The Divine Dance*. New Kensington, PA: Whitaker House, 2016.

Ryrie, Charles Caldwell. *The Ryrie Study Bible: NIV*. Chicago, IL: Moody Press, 1986.

The Episcopal Church. *Book of Common Prayer*. Kindport, TN: Seabury Press, 1976.

Viola, Frank. *Reimaging Church: Pursuing the Dream of Organic Christianity*. Colorado Springs, CO: David C. Cook, 2008.

Young, William Paul. *The Shack*. Newbury Park, CA: Windblown Media, 2007.

About the Author

David G. Frantz is a retired senior international energy and financial executive. His career involved structuring and financing utility-scale energy projects all over the world. A former US Naval officer, he served in combat during the Vietnam conflict. Originally from Warren, Pennsylvania, he now resides with his wife, Claudia, in Williamsburg, Virginia.